DODGEBALL

by Michael Decker

The Greater World of Sports

SportsZone

An Imprint of Abdo Publishing | abdobooks.com

abdobooks.com

Published by Abdo Publishing, a division of ABDO, PO Box 398166, Minneapolis, Minnesota 55439. Copyright © 2020 by Abdo Consulting Group, Inc. International copyrights reserved in all countries. No part of this book may be reproduced in any form without written permission from the publisher. SportsZone™ is a trademark and logo of Abdo Publishing.

Printed in the United States of America, North Mankato, Minnesota
092019
012020

THIS BOOK CONTAINS
RECYCLED MATERIALS

Cover Photos: iStockphoto, right; Michael Burrell/iStockphoto, left
Interior Photos: iStockphoto, 5, 12, 17, 18; Randy Hoeft/Yuma Sun/AP Images, 6, 8; Shutterstock Images, 7; Universal History Archive/Universal Images Group/Getty Images, 11; Red Line Editorial, 14; Richard Lautens/Toronto Star/Getty Images, 20, 22–23; Warren Dillaway/The Star-Beacon/AP Images, 24; Bret Hartman/Boys & Girls Clubs of America/AP Images, 25; Jae C. Hong/AP Images, 26; Syariff Hidayatullah/Shutterstock Images, 28

Editor: Melissa York
Series Designer: Melissa Martin

Library of Congress Control Number: 2019941976

Publisher's Cataloging-in-Publication Data

Names: Decker, Michael, author
Title: Dodgeball / by Michael Decker
Description: Minneapolis, Minnesota : Abdo Publishing, 2020 | Series: The greater world of sports | Includes online resources and index
Identifiers: ISBN 9781532190384 (lib. bdg.) | ISBN 9781532176234 (ebook)
Subjects: LCSH: Dodgeball--Juvenile literature. | Ball games--Juvenile literature. | Team games--Juvenile literature. | Outdoor games--Juvenile literature. | Sports--Juvenile literature.
Classification: DDC 796.3--dc23

TABLE OF CONTENTS

Chapter 1

TIME TO PLAY

The two teams line up on separate sides of the gym, ready to play. The two opposing teams wear red and blue shirts. The only thing between the red team and the blue team are a set of balls lined up on the center line. Unlike most team sports, dodgeball doesn't require any other equipment.

The referee blows her whistle. The players all sprint toward the center line. It's a quick dash to see who can get to the balls first. A few players from the red team each grab a ball off the ground. Then, they slowly start backpedaling away from the center line.

Players have to hustle to grab a ball at the start of a dodgeball game.

Players who don't have a ball must be quick dodgers or they will be out.

The players who grabbed balls scan the other side. The players who don't have balls quickly shuffle from side to side. They glance warily at their opponents, getting ready to dive out of the way of an incoming ball.

Players employ different strategies. One girl on the red team wants to go after the best players on the blue team first. She keeps her eyes on them at all times. Another boy on the blue team grabs two balls. He's going to use them to block any throws that come his way.

A red team player launches a ball across the center line. The ball heads toward a blue team

Players try to catch the balls to get their opponents out.

player's foot. He leaps in the air and the ball misses him as it bounces past. The boy collects the ball and fires it back. The ball strikes the red team player on the hip. The player is out of the game.

Dodgeball players practice many athletic skills.

8

Then, another blue team player whips a ball to the other side. A red team player leaps in the air and catches it with both hands. The blue team player is out.

Soon, only one player remains on each side. They each hold a ball. Suddenly the red player throws his ball at the last opponent. The ball strikes her on the knee. That ends the game.

The players who were out of the game run onto the floor. Both teams' players high-five and shake hands.

People started playing dodgeball as we know it over 100 years ago. Since then, it's become a popular game in the United States. Many people start playing as kids, but it's a game for all ages.

Chapter 2

THE HISTORY OF DODGEBALL

Children around the world have played with balls since ancient times. The ball is one of the oldest kinds of toys. Just like children today, kids thousands of years ago played throwing and dodging games.

Dodgeball with modern rules started around 1900. At that time, schools and parks started building playgrounds. They had play structures and athletic fields, and some even had swimming pools. Many people lived in big cities. Parents wanted safe places for kids to play, exercise, make friends, and learn teamwork. These playgrounds had adults watching, and they taught kids rules

As new playgrounds were built around 1900, teachers and children made up new games to play there.

for many games and sports. One of these sports was dodgeball.

Emmett Dunn Angell taught gym teachers at the University of Wisconsin, Harvard, and Yale. He was part of a group of teachers who believed play was an important part of all children's education. He wrote a book about playground games, including dodgeball, in 1910. Dodgeball was already popular at this time, and other books from the era included variations of the game.

In his description of the game, one team made a circle. They had one ball, a leather basketball. The other team stood inside. They were called dodgers. Members of the outside team threw the ball at the dodgers to get them out. When all the dodgers got out, the teams switched. A teacher timed the game, and the dodging team that lasted longest won.

Hard leather balls made early dodgeball a painful game to play.

DODGEBALL COURT

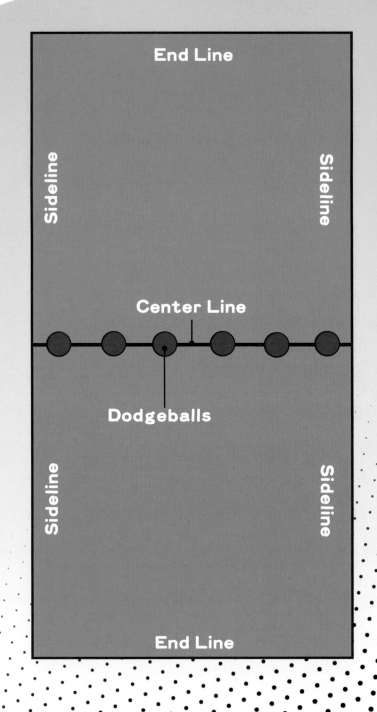

The game changed over time. The red rubber playground ball was invented in the 1940s. It bounced, and when it hit a person it hurt less than a hard basketball. That made dodgeball more fun. Eventually, the rules evolved to include multiple balls. They were lined up on the center line, and players ran to grab them at the start of the game. Modern dodgeball was born.

Chapter 3

THE ABCs OF DODGEBALL

The most important equipment in dodgeball is the ball. Often players use rubber balls that are about 8 inches (20 cm) around. But these balls can hurt people if they are thrown too hard. Because of that, many people now use softer balls. They are made of materials such as foam or cloth. Besides the balls, there is no other equipment. Players can wear what they like. Many wear a t-shirt and athletic shorts. Some teams have uniforms.

Dodgeball is most often played inside. The court is usually the size of a volleyball court or basketball court. It features a center line that

All you really need to play dodgeball is some balls. Many prefer soft foam balls.

It is also possible to play dodgeball outside.

divides the two teams. There is a sideline where players go when they are out of the game.

Each team starts on its own side of the court. All of the balls are lined up along the center line. The number of balls can differ based on how many people are playing.

Sometimes, a referee or teacher is on hand to enforce the rules of the game. If there is a referee, he or she will signal when the game starts.

Once the game starts, players rush to the middle of the court to grab the ball. Players can begin throwing the balls at each other right away. There are usually four ways to get out. Players who step over the center line are out. Players who are hit by a ball are out. When an opponent catches a ball, the player who threw it is out. Finally, a player may try to block a throw with a ball in her hands. But if she drops the ball while blocking with it, she's out.

Changing the Rules

There are many rule variations that can change certain parts of a dodgeball game. A time limit for the game may be set ahead of time. Sometimes there are penalties for players who hold onto the ball for too long and don't throw it. Many dodgeball games don't allow players to throw the ball at an opponent's head.

Once a player is out, he heads to the sideline. Players line up in the order in which they left the game. If a player catches a ball thrown by an opponent, the player who has been out the longest can return to the game. The game ends when one side has no players left.

A player who blocks a thrown ball with another ball is not out. Players can hold multiple balls at a time.

Chapter 4

MAKING DODGEBALL FUN

Though dodgeball is often a fun sport, it can hurt people physically and mentally. Some people say they stopped playing the sport because of bad experiences in school. Some kids felt like they were picked on during dodgeball. Others were hurt physically by a hard throw.

But kids continue to play the sport at many elementary schools. Some teachers believe dodgeball helps kids to develop throwing skills. Players spin, twist, and work on their sense of balance.

Dodgeball can be a painful game.

23

Kids practice athletic moves and learn strategy and awareness while playing dodgeball.

They practice strategy. The game also trains them to be aware of their surroundings.

Teachers just want to make sure kids are having fun while playing and no one feels targeted. It can help a team win if all members choose one opponent to target at the same time. But it is not good sportsmanship because that opponent doesn't get a fair chance to dodge.

Many older people enjoy playing dodgeball. Many colleges have dodgeball leagues for students. Some students even travel and play teams from other schools. Many organizations

People of all ages can enjoy dodgeball.

and schools hold dodgeball games for charity. Players compete in games to raise money for a cause. In 2012, students at the University of California, Irvine, set the world record for the largest dodgeball game. They gathered more than 6,000 people to throw countless balls at each other.

The National Dodgeball League began in 2004. It includes teams from all over the United States. In 2012, the World Dodgeball Federation formed. This organization puts together international tournaments. Countries compete against each other to see which team is the best in the world.

On the Big Screen

In 2004 dodgeball hit the big screen in the movie *Dodgeball: A True Underdog Story*. The movie is about a man struggling to keep his local gym open. He learns about a dodgeball tournament in which the winning team gets $50,000. The owner puts together a team featuring some of the gym's members. Working together, the team wins the tournament and saves the gym.

UC Irvine students set the world record for the largest dodgeball game two years in a row, in 2011 and 2012.

Dodgeball is a simple game, but that doesn't mean it's easy. Players develop their throwing and catching skills and work on their fitness. But most of all, they can expect to have fun. That's why dodgeball continues to be a popular sport for people of all ages.

Dodgeball teams work together and have fun.

GLOSSARY

backpedal

To move backward in a quick fashion.

charity

An organization that raises money for those in need.

equipment

The items necessary to play a certain sport.

league

A group of teams that participate together in a sport.

sideline

The area on the court where players go when they are eliminated from the game.

strategy

A plan of action to achieve a certain goal.

target

An object of attention or an attack.

MORE INFORMATION

BOOKS

London, Martha. *Pickleball*. Minneapolis, MN: Abdo Publishing, 2020.

Marthaler, Jon. *Offbeat Sports*. Minneapolis, MN: Abdo Publishing, 2018.

ONLINE RESOURCES

To learn more about dodgeball, please visit abdobooklinks.com or scan this QR code. These links are routinely monitored and updated to provide the most current information available.

INDEX

ABOUT THE AUTHOR

Michael Decker has spent his career as a children's book author, writing about various topics. He lives in Wyoming.